DULVERTON
Df

Francis Frith's
SOMERSET

PHOTOGRAPHIC MEMORIES

Francis Frith's
SOMERSET

Martin Andrew

First published in the United Kingdom in 2000 by
Frith Book Company Ltd

Paperback Edition 2004
ISBN 1-85937-944-3

British Library Cataloguing in Publication Data

Francis Frith's Somerset - Photographic Memories
Martin Andrew
ISBN 1-85937-944-3

Frith Book Company Ltd
Frith's Barn, Teffont,
Salisbury, Wiltshire SP3 5QP
Tel: +44 (0) 1722 716 376
Fax: +44 (0) 1722 716 881
Email: info@francisfrith.co.uk
Web Site: www.francisfrith.co.uk

Printed and bound in Great Britain

The colour-tinting is for illustrative purposes only, and is not intended to be historically accurate

Front Cover: Dulverton, Lions Hotel 1896 37653t

Contents

FRANCIS FRITH: *Victorian Pioneer*

FRANCIS FRITH, Victorian founder of the world-famous photographic archive, was a complex and fascinating man. A devout Quaker and a highly successful Victorian businessman, he was both philosophical by nature and pioneering in outlook.

By 1855 Francis Frith had already established a wholesale grocery business in Liverpool, and sold it for the astonishing sum of £200,000, which is the equivalent today of over £15,000,000. Now a multi-millionaire, he was able to indulge his passion for travel. As a child he had pored over travel books written by early explorers, and his fancy and imagination had been stirred by family holidays to the sublime mountain regions of Wales and Scotland. 'What a land of spirit-stirring and enriching scenes and places!' he had written. He was to return to these scenes of grandeur in later years to 'recapture the thousands of vivid and tender memories', but with a different purpose. Now in his thirties, and captivated by the new science of photography, Frith set out on a series of pioneering journeys to the Nile regions that occupied him from 1856 until 1860.

INTRIGUE AND ADVENTURE

He took with him on his travels a specially-designed wicker carriage that acted as both dark-room and sleeping chamber. These far-flung journeys were packed with intrigue and adventure. In his life story, written when he was sixty-three, Frith tells of being held captive by bandits, and of fighting 'an awful midnight battle to the very point of surrender with a deadly pack of hungry, wild dogs'. Sporting flowing Arab costume, Frith arrived at Akaba by camel sixty years before Lawrence, where he encountered 'desert princes and rival sheikhs, blazing with jewel-hilted swords'.

During these extraordinary adventures he was assiduously exploring the desert regions bordering the Nile and patiently recording the antiquities and peoples with his camera. He was the first photographer to venture beyond the sixth cataract. Africa was still the mysterious 'Dark Continent', and Stanley and Livingstone's historic meeting was a decade into the future. The conditions for picture taking confound belief. He laboured for hours in his wicker dark-room in the sweltering heat of the desert, while the volatile chemicals fizzed dangerously in their trays. Often he was forced to work in remote tombs and caves where conditions were cooler. Back in London he exhibited his photographs and was 'rapturously cheered' by members of the Royal Society. His reputation as a photographer was made overnight. An eminent modern historian has likened their impact on the population of the time to that on our own generation of the first photographs taken on the surface of the moon.

VENTURE OF A LIFE-TIME

Characteristically, Frith quickly spotted the opportunity to create a new business as a specialist publisher of photographs. He lived in an era of immense and sometimes violent change. For the poor in the early part of Victoria's reign work was a drudge and the hours long, and people had precious little free time to enjoy themselves.

Most had no transport other than a cart or gig at their disposal, and had not travelled far beyond the boundaries of their own town or village. However, by the 1870s, the railways had threaded their way across the country, and Bank Holidays and half-day Saturdays had been made obligatory by Act of Parliament. All of a sudden the ordinary working man and his family were able to enjoy days out and see a little more of the world.

With characteristic business acumen, Francis Frith foresaw that these new tourists would enjoy having souvenirs to commemorate their days out. In 1860 he married Mary Ann Rosling and set out with the intention of photographing every city, town and village in Britain. For the next thirty years he travelled the country by train and by pony and trap, producing fine photographs of seaside resorts and beauty spots that were keenly bought by millions of Victorians. These prints were painstakingly pasted into family albums and pored over during the dark nights of winter, rekindling precious memories of summer excursions.

THE RISE OF FRITH & CO

Frith's studio was soon supplying retail shops all over the country. To meet the demand he gathered about him a small team of photographers, and published the work of independent artist-photographers of the calibre of Roger Fenton and Francis Bedford. In order to gain some understanding of the scale of Frith's business one only has to look at the catalogue issued by Frith & Co in 1886: it

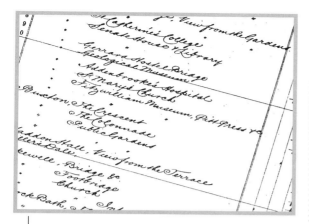

runs to some 670 pages, listing not only many thousands of views of the British Isles but also many photographs of most European countries, and China, Japan, the USA and Canada – note the sample page shown above from the hand-written *Frith & Co* ledgers detailing pictures taken. By 1890 Frith had created the greatest specialist photographic publishing company in the world, with over 2,000 outlets – more than the combined number that Boots and WH Smith have today! The picture on the right shows the *Frith & Co* display board at Ingleton in the Yorkshire Dales. Beautifully constructed with mahogany frame and gilt inserts, it could display up to a dozen local scenes.

POSTCARD BONANZA

The ever-popular holiday postcard we know today took many years to develop. In 1870 the Post Office issued the first plain cards, with a pre-printed stamp on one face. In 1894 they allowed other publishers' cards to be sent through the mail with an attached adhesive halfpenny stamp. Demand grew rapidly, and in 1895 a new size of postcard

was permitted called the court card, but there was little room for illustration. In 1899, a year after Frith's death, a new card measuring 5.5 x 3.5 inches became the standard format, but it was not until 1902 that the divided back came into being, with address and message on one face and a full-size illustration on the other. *Frith & Co* were in the vanguard of postcard development, and Frith's sons Eustace and Cyril continued their father's monumental task, expanding the number of views offered to the public and recording more and more places in Britain, as the coasts and countryside were opened up to mass travel.

Francis Frith died in 1898 at his villa in Cannes, his great project still growing. The archive he created continued in business for another seventy years. By 1970 it contained over a third of a million pictures of 7,000 cities, towns and villages. The massive photographic record Frith has left to us stands as a living monument to a special and very remarkable man.

Frith's Archive: *A Unique Legacy*

FRANCIS FRITH'S legacy to us today is of immense significance and value, for the magnificent archive of evocative photographs he created provides a unique record of change in 7,000 cities, towns and villages throughout Britain over a century and more. Frith and his fellow studio photographers revisited locations many times down the years to update their views, compiling for us an enthralling and colourful pageant of British life and character.

We tend to think of Frith's sepia views of Britain as nostalgic, for most of us use them to conjure up memories of places in our own lives with which we have family associations. It often makes us forget that to Francis Frith they were records of daily life as it was actually being lived in the cities, towns and

villages of his day. The Victorian age was one of great and often bewildering change for ordinary people, and though the pictures evoke an impression of slower times, life was as busy and hectic as it is today.

We are fortunate that Frith was a photographer of the people, dedicated to recording the minutiae of everyday life. For it is this sheer wealth of visual data, the painstaking chronicle of changes in dress, transport, street layouts, buildings, housing, engineering and landscape that captivates us so much today. His remarkable images offer us a powerful link with the past and with the lives of our ancestors.

TODAY'S TECHNOLOGY

Computers have now made it possible for Frith's many thousands of images to be accessed almost instantly. In the Frith archive today, each photograph is carefully 'digitised' then stored on a CD Rom. Frith archivists can locate a single photograph amongst thousands within seconds. Views can be catalogued and sorted under a variety of categories of place and content to the immediate benefit of researchers. Inexpensive reference prints can be created for them at the touch of a mouse button, and a wide range of books and other printed materials assembled and published for a wider, more general readership - in the next twelve months over a hundred Frith local history titles will be published! The day-to-

See Frith at www.francisfrith.co.uk

day workings of the archive are very different from how they were in Francis Frith's time: imagine the herculean task of sorting through eleven tons of glass negatives as Frith had to do to locate a particular sequence of pictures! Yet the archive still prides itself on maintaining the same high standards of excellence laid down by Francis Frith, including the painstaking cataloguing and indexing of every view.

It is curious to reflect on how the internet now allows researchers in America and elsewhere greater instant access to the archive than Frith himself ever enjoyed. Many thousands of individual views can be called up on screen within seconds on one of the Frith internet sites, enabling people living continents away to revisit the streets of their ancestral home town, or view places in Britain where they have enjoyed holidays. Many overseas researchers welcome the chance to view special theme selections, such as transport, sports, costume and ancient monuments.

We are certain that Francis Frith would have heartily approved of these modern developments, for he himself was always working at the very limits of Victorian photographic technology.

THE VALUE OF THE ARCHIVE TODAY

Because of the benefits brought by the computer, Frith's images are increasingly studied by social historians, by researchers into genealogy and ancestory, by architects, town planners, and by teachers and schoolchildren involved in local history projects. In addition, the archive offers every one of us a unique opportunity to examine the places where we and our families have lived and worked down the years. Immensely successful in Frith's own era, the archive is now, a century and more on, entering a new phase of popularity.

THE PAST IN TUNE WITH THE FUTURE

Historians consider the Francis Frith Collection to be of prime national importance. It is the only archive of its kind remaining in private ownership and has been valued at a million pounds. However, this figure is now rapidly increasing as digital technology enables more and more people around the world to enjoy its benefits.

Francis Frith's archive is now housed in an historic timber barn in the beautiful village of Teffont in Wiltshire. Its founder would not recognize the archive office as it is today. In place of the many thousands of dusty boxes containing glass plate negatives and an all-pervading odour of photographic chemicals, there are now ranks of computer screens. He would be amazed to watch his images travelling round the world at unimaginable speeds through network and internet lines.

The archive's future is both bright and exciting. Francis Frith, with his unshakeable belief in making photographs available to the greatest number of people, would undoubtedly approve of what is being done today with his lifetime's work. His photographs, depicting our shared past, are now bringing pleasure and enlightenment to millions around the world a century and more after his death.

SOMERSET - *An Introduction*

FOR MANY YEARS my wife and I used to stay with friends who lived in a cottage near Churchstanton in the heart of the Blackdown Hills. From there we explored west Somerset, and when they moved to Stoke sub Hamdon we got to know east Somerset as well. Stoke sub Hamdon could not have been a better location: it lies in the lee of Ham Hill's pockmarked old quarries that produced a wonderful golden buff oolitic limestone used everywhere in the area. From these trips we came to appreciate a county that many pass through on their way to Devon and Cornwall. Possibly they come down the M5, which crosses the vast Somerset Levels, the flat expanses of central Somerset that mislead the casual tourist into comparing the county with, say, Lincolnshire.

However, like Lincolnshire, there is much more to it than drained marshes: Somerset is a county of great beauty and variety in its roughly 70 miles from east to west and 30 from north to south. Its northern boundary is the Bristol Channel, and in the south it comes to within seven miles of the English Channel. This book is divided into five chapters, each with particular geographical themes. It does not include the areas north of the Mendip Hills which were annexed to the County of Avon, now defunct and not lamented. It means, of course, that what was north-east Somerset is to be found elsewhere in the companion volumes of the Frith series, such as 'Around Bath' or 'Around Bristol'.

Somerset is remarkably unspoilt, and still predominantly rural in feel, with a large

number of small market towns and something of a predominance of pastoral farming. This is always a good thing scenically, for hedges are not grubbed up with nearly as much eagerness and fields remain small. Much of the county is also pretty well wooded. But I cannot generalise too far, for Somerset cannot be understood without reference to its varied geology and its striking scenic effects. In essence, the county consists of a flat centre surrounded by hills: clockwise from the north-east they are the Mendips, the southern limestone hills, the Blackdown Hills, Exmoor and the Quantocks. The best building stones come from the southern limestone hills, which are in effect a geological extension of the Cotswolds.

As ever, the geology of an area influences its buildings. Somerset is very fortunate to have the oolitic limestone of Ham Hill; hereabouts whole towns and villages are built in it, often entirely as dressed stone rather than thin rubble. In hues of golden buff to brown, Montacute is perhaps the best town and country house to visit to see this wonderful stone at its best. Parallel with the oolitic limestone are the Lias limestones, usually blue-grey, grey or white; they are used extensively, usually as rubble stone, in towns such as Bruton. The Lias stone extends north-west from the southern hills to form the Polden Hills, a spine of hills that cuts the Moors or Levels in two north-west of Street.

These limestones are relatively young in geological terms, but there are far more ancient limestones in the county. These are the carboniferous limestones of the Mendip Hills, a much harder stone, normally used as a rubble stone. Scenically, the Mendips produce by far the most awesome landscape in Somerset: Cheddar Gorge. In the west of Somerset, different and more ancient rock produces different building materials. A band of sandstone runs west of Taunton, a beautiful stone that can be used as a dressed stone as well as a rubble. The Quantocks and Exmoor yield hard Old Red Sandstones and slates, difficult to work and used mostly as rubble in thin beds. The Levels and Moors and the lower land produces brick; cob or earth wall construction is found across the whole of southern Somerset and Exmoor, nearly always rendered and colourwashed. Indeed, the characteristic vernacular architecture of the limestone and sandstone areas is farms and villages of whitewashed cottages under thatched roofs, the whitewash concealing either rubble stone or cob.

So these rocks of Somerset provide the materials for the regional vernacular buildings, but what landscape do these rocks produce? In the north-west, Exmoor is of

course quite the wildest and most barren part of the county; its sandstones, slates, shales and limestones are of marginal agricultural use. Exmoor's tops are good only for sheep, hardy Exmoor ponies and forestry, and gorse, bracken and heather abound. However, surrounding it to the north are steep well-wooded cliffs and combes rising sharply from the sea, while to the east streams and rivers have cut deep valleys and combes, which are also well-wooded and lush: a complete contrast to the plateau. The towns, villages and hamlets occupy these valleys, such as Winsford or Dulverton, the latter now the headquarters of the Exmoor National Park Authority. The highest point is Dunkery Beacon at 1705 feet, but much of the moor is around the 1500 feet mark. It is a very beautiful but wild area; much is made of the 'Lorna Doone' connection, the novel by R D Blackmore set in Exmoor.

The Quantocks, east of Exmoor, are in some respects an outlier of it. About twelve miles long, much steeper on the west scarp, they are also topped with heather, gorse and bracken. More undulating than Exmoor, their highest point is Will's Neck at 1260 feet. Picturesque hamlets and villages cling to the western and southern foothills linked by narrow hedged and winding lanes. Beyond the Levels, the Mendips rise spectacularly steeply from the plain to a plateau roughly 1000 feet high; the highest point is Beacon Batch above Burrington at 1066 feet. On the tops, dry stone walls divide fields of thin sheep pasture. The astonishingly steep-sided and awesomely grand Cheddar Gorge is particularly striking, but there are also numerous caves and caverns, a common feature of carboniferous limestone country; Wookey Hole is a cavern the public can visit.

There are also further carboniferous outcrops, including Brean Hill and the island of Steep Holm in the Bristol Channel. Indeed, one of the most remarkable features of the flat lands of Somerset is the propensity for geology to interfere: there are numerous knolls, tors and outliers dotted around the levels, from the most famous one, the numinous Glastonbury Tor, to Brent Knoll. The Levels or Moors, divided by the Polden Hills, occupy a huge swathe of the centre of the county. Marshland and peat swamp, the Levels were systematically drained; narrow rectangular fields were formed, with drainage ditches on all sides feeding into embanked rivers or drains such as the King's Sedgemoor Drain or the Huntspill River. The process got under way properly in the Middle Ages. The Abbots of Glastonbury, who owned much of the marshes, played a leading role in a process that took hundreds of years.

Pollarded willows were planted by the thousand, and many of these survive along these drainage ditches called 'rhines'. Wherever the ground rises above the Moors settlement took place, linked by lanes zig-zagging around the field edges. Peat extraction in some areas takes place, but the chief use of the flat, drained landscape is pastoral, with sheep and cattle grazing as far as the eye can see.

Further south, the lush Vale of Taunton Deane is more rolling countryside with pasture, arable and cider apple orchards to supply one of Somerset's most famous industries. The Vale shades into the Blackdown Hills to the south-west, characterised by intimate valleys and small fields in rolling hills, and into the limestone hills to the south. Here Somerset's great wealth from medieval times to the early 19th century was found: the sheep whose wool fed the cloth industries and markets of towns like Shepton Mallet or Frome.

This beautiful county has had a long history, and this introduction can merely touch upon it. No mention of the county's early history - or rather pre-history - should omit the ancient trackways, some datable to 4000 BC , that linked higher islands of settlement in the marshes of the Levels. The most famous is the Sweet Track: a stretch has

been reconstructed in Shapwick Heath Nature Reserve. The Iron Age also left its mark, with hill forts greatly varying in size. That at Brent Knoll is made more dramatic by its location on top of a very steep hill which rises out of the plain, but they are scattered over the hills of the county, such as that on Dundon Hill, south of Street, or Hamdon Hill; but the most well known must be Cadbury Castle west of Wincanton, attributed in folklore to King Arthur's Camelot.

The Roman occupation had its greatest effect on Bath, beyond the scope of this collection. The Fosse Way, the great Roman road from Lincoln to Axminster across the Devon border, passed through the county via Bath and Ilchester, at the time called Lendiniae and a tribal capital. There were numerous villas of the Romanised local landowners and farmers, but it was after the Roman legions left in around 410 AD that Somerset came to legendary prominence. Glastonbury has long been associated with King Arthur, a British king or general who fought the Saxon invaders in the 5th century. He was successful enough to slow down the conquest significantly, but there is little or no evidence that he was more than a local warlord or general somewhere in the west in locations varying from Cumbria to Cornwall. It is good to think of Glastonbury as the Isle of

Avalon, rising above the marshes, but the Arthurian legend is just that, despite exhaustive researches. Archaeologists dug into Cadbury Castle, further east, to see if it could have been Arthur's Camelot, but reached no firm conclusion.

Somerset comes into verifiable history with the Danish invasions of the 8th century. These were so successful that the King of Wessex lost all his kingdom to the east of Somerset for a while, and Mercia was completely overrun. King Alfred retreated to the marshes of central Somerset in 878; he fortified the Isle of Athelney as his base, from which he gathered armies and waged successful war against Guthrum, the Danish leader, and recovered his kingdom. There is a monument on the spot where his base is supposed to have been at Athelney, south of Bridgwater. The Anglo-Saxon Chronicle reports all this, and tells of the heathen Guthrum's subsequent baptism at Aller, which was followed by feasting at Alfred's royal residence in Wedmore. The subsequent Treaty of Wedmore divided England into two: the Danes were ceded all north and east of Watling Street, while Alfred effectively saved Wessex.

The Middle Ages saw the hills of the south prosper with wool production and cloth making. Numerous market towns developed, some, like Chard, laid out in the 13th century, others with markets added to existing settlements, such as Somerton. Certainly, more market crosses survive in Somerset than anywhere else, and the towns are mostly architecturally enjoyable, although Yeovil has suffered more reconstruction and alteration than others. Somerset's genteel decline after the wool industry moved to Yorkshire and Lancashire factories after 1800 was beneficial in fact, for their character as market towns conserve more of their Georgian and early 19th-century character than many comparable sized ones in more successful areas. In fact, Yeovil's economic success was its historic architecture's worst enemy. The wool trade also resulted in numerous very fine churches, particularly in the 15th century when trade was at its zenith. The chief glory of Somerset churches are their towers, which developed a style recognisable enough to be called 'Somerset Towers'.

Village architecture is more varied, but there is a distinct style of whitewashed render or rubble with thatched roofs; the older houses have an external chimney stack at the mid point of the front wall. These are characteristic of Devon and Dorset as well, but the visitor knows that he will find beautiful villages here. I have said nothing of industry, beyond mentioning quarrying of stone: there

was also mining, such as the iron ore extracted from the Brendon Hills and shipped via Watchet. Bridgwater roof tiles are well-known; Yeovil has in this century become the home of the Westland Aircraft Company, and Clark's Shoes dominate Street. Generally speaking, however, Somerset is not a heavily-industrialised county - to its visual benefit, no doubt.

Leisure and tourism have a long history. Bath has always been popular, and sea water bathing led to the development of seaside resorts in the 19th century such as Weston-super-Mare, Burnham-on-Sea and Minehead, aided by the arrival of the railway to bring the holiday makers in. Steam trains reached Weston in 1848, Burnham in 1858 and Minehead in 1874. Cheddar Gorge and Wookey Hole, Wells, Glastonbury and Bath are the most popular tourist spots, as well as Dunster and Exmoor, of course.

The chapters in this book divide Somerset into five areas, occasionally a little arbitrarily, designed as routes that the reader can follow one at a time or in sequence. It is a large county, and to do it anything like justice you would probably be best advised not to try to do more than one route in a day: even that might be a tough challenge, and the chapters could be further broken down. The first chapter starts in the county town, Taunton,

and heads off into Exmoor, and from Porlock heads to the Quantocks before returning to Taunton. Chapter two takes seaside Somerset as its theme, and follows the coast from Minehead to Brean Down: something of a mixed bag, with seaside resorts of varying quality, such as Burnham on Sea or Brean, mingling with showpieces like Dunster. The third chapter is a tour of the Mendips, which includes the cathedral city of Wells and heads east to the Frome area. Chapter four covers the Levels, starting at Bridgwater and following a southern sweep to Glastonbury, and the last chapter crosses the southern part of the county from east near Bruton to west, finishing at Ilminster.

I enjoyed working out and following the routes in a county of very great physical beauty, not only in terms of landscape but also in terms of the architecture of its villages, towns and farms. Who could forget their first sight of the towering crags along the Cheddar Gorge, or the beauty of a village like Luccombe: whitewash and thatch and a tall-towered stone church nestling in a fold of the landscape, sheep and cattle grazing small fields all around, with the wooded backdrop of the edge of Exmoor? Somerset is a truly rewarding county that carries its architectural heritage lightly amid great scenic quality.

Taunton, Exmoor & The Quantocks

TAUNTON

EAST STREET 1902 48724

The first chapter's tour starts in the heart of the lush Vale of Taunton Deane in the county town of Taunton, a bustling town with much of its former through traffic taken by the nearby M5. Here, East Street heads towards Fore Street past 1830s stucco terraces. The Claridges London Hotel is now occupied by Waterstones bookshop and Marks and Spencers.

TAUNTON
FORE STREET 1902 48723
Fore Street and the triangular medieval market place are the heart of the town: here we see the south side, behind the Market House's stand of horse-drawn cabs. Apart from The Stores, most of the buildings survive, including the Tudor Tavern with its exuberant timber-framing and shown here advertising Anglo-Bavarian Ales and Stouts. These gabled houses are survivors of the 1645 destruction of the town during the Civil War.

TAUNTON, FORE STREET 1902 48720

Much has changed here: the trams have long gone, the Celtic cross memorial to the Somerset Light Infantry's Burma Campaign in the 1880s is now a traffic island further up in North Street, while the open market arcades attached to the 1770s Market House were replaced by buildings in 1932. Taunton was also proud of its early electric street lights installed in 1886.

TAUNTON, ST MARY'S CHURCH 1888 20858

Hammet Street, with its brick terrace houses, was laid out in 1788 off North Street, focusing on the magnificent late 15th-century tower of St Mary's church. This was entirely rebuilt in 1862, having become dangerous. It is sad that the houses on the left have been replaced. Behind the cameraman lie the castle remains, outside whose gates the medieval market town was established.

TAUNTON, THE COUNTY CRICKET GROUND 1902 48716
The headquarters of Somerset County Cricket Club, founded in 1875, lie on the south bank of the River Tone; although the grandstands are much changed, the arched one still in essence survives. Beyond are the town's two superb 'Somerset style' Perpendicular Gothic church towers, St Mary's beyond the (now demolished) factory chimney and St James' Church to the right, also a 19th-century rebuild.

BATHPOOL, THE BRIDGE 1902 48745
A radically transformed settlement now, with the bridge long rebuilt, Bathpool is just off the modern road built to link the town with the M5's Junction 25. The village lies just beyond where it crosses the A38 Bristol road at a vast roundabout.

BISHOP'S HULL, THE VILLAGE 1906 55810
Now in effect a suburb of Taunton, the village is still distinctly a village architecturally, with its 1586 Elizabethan manor house, recently freshly yellow ochre colourwashed. The church of St Peter and St Paul is also unusual - it has one of Somerset's octagonal towers. In 1826 the medieval nave was drastically altered into a barn-like preaching box. Since 1906, the cottage on the left has gone, and the church porch has been rebuilt.

WELLINGTON, THE SQUARE 1912 64490
Wellington, about ten miles south-west of Taunton at the foot of the Blackdown Hills, is an attractive market town with its focus where South, Fore and High Streets meet. Here the late Regency Town Hall was built in 1833 with its cupola and clocks; the latter have since been replaced by square faced ones. The splendid E H Aycliffe shopfronts to the left have since been replaced.

WELLINGTON, FORE STREET 1912 64491

The Town Hall, also built as a corn market, was opened by the Duke of Wellington in 1833; a 173 feet obelisk monument to the Duke is on Wellington Hill to the south of the town. Indeed, Arthur Wellesley, the victor of Waterloo, took his title from this Somerset town. Most of Shaplands Hotel beyond on the left has been demolished for a rather nasty supermarket building.

WELLINGTON, FORE STREET 1938 88415

By 1938, Shaplands Restaurant has become a Cafe, and the hotel had expanded into the shops on the right. Since then the hotel has been demolished, leaving only the Gregory and Brean bay on the left. As can be seen in this view, Fore Street exhibited a rather heterogeneous range of architectural styles.

WELLINGTON
SOUTH STREET 1907 58726
South Street, however, showed more architectural consistency than Fore Street, or even High Street. Grattons, on the right, was replaced in the 1920s by the Midland Bank seen in photograph No 88415, now of course the HSBC bank. Behind the photographer is the Town Hall, which closes the vista up South Street.

WESTFORD, THE CLOTH MILLS 1907 58737

WESTFORD
The Cloth Mills 1907

A mile west of Wellington, Westford was a mill village with large cloth mills along the River Tone. Here the photographer looks towards a range of 19th-century industrial buildings, all of which survive, although not now in mill use. The one on the right is now a coal merchants, while the whitewashed one has lost the cupola whose bell summoned the mill hands to their work.

HALSE
The Village c1955

Moving north, deeper into the Vale of Taunton Deane, we reach the cob or earth wall country, where whitewashed rendered cottages with thatched roofs become common. There is still plenty of stone, although not the wonderful golden oolitic limestones from Ham Hill and the far south of the county; here we have the Blue Lias, a thin limestone which can only be used for rubble walling.

HALSE, THE VILLAGE c1955 H498505

HALSE, THE VILLAGE c1955 H498504

Here the huntsman and his pack of beagles pass Manor Cottage and School Cottage with the main body of the hunt behind them: and at this time, there was not a sign of a hunt saboteur. The boundary walls on the left are in Blue Lias rubble stone left unpainted, while the lean-to at the left of Manor Cottage behind the huntsman has its rubble thickly limewashed.

WATERROW, THE HAMLET c1955 W579009

Climbing westwards, the Taunton to Barnstaple road crosses the well-treed and young River Tone Valley at Waterrow. From the road we look across the garden of riverside Tonecroft along the steep-sided valley of a tributary stream that descends from Heydon Hill. Rock Cottage, on the left, has had its render removed to expose the thin-bedded ancient Devonian sandstone rubble used for building on Exmoor and the western hills of Somerset.

DULVERTON, GENERAL VIEW 1892 31173
Turning north into the upper Exe valley, we enter the Exmoor National Park at Dulverton, on the Exford Road in the tributary valley of the River Barle. The old workhouse is now the headquarters of the National Park Authority. In this view the medieval bridge is on the left and the former Crepe Mill of 1814, now the Dulverton Laundry, dominates the centre.

WINSFORD, THE VILLAGE 1892 31191
Climbing up from Dulverton the road crosses typical sheep-grazed Exmoor moorland, bright with yellow gorse flowers and heather, before descending into Winsford in the upper Exe valley. This delightful village of whitewashed cottages focused on a stream has changed little; the tall pine tree has gone, but its stone-walled surround remains. The Royal Oak now has its porches and lean-tos thatched, as well as the main roof.

WINSFORD
The Village 1930

By 1930 a War Memorial has appeared, while the cottage beyond, Old Tythe, then the post office, is now no longer a shop. The bridge over the stream in the foreground is an ancient stone slab or 'clapper' bridge; there are many of these in Exmoor, including the famous Tarr Steps across the River Barle, five miles away over Winsford Hill.

———

EXFORD
Park Street 1892

North-west from Winsford we reach Exford, where the River Exe is but a stream. This village is virtually the creation of its 19th-century rector, Joseph Relph, who built large numbers of houses to double its size, including Tarrs Inn, which we can see in this view, with its large sash windows. This was itself rebuilt around 1900 as the Crown Hotel in an Arts and Crafts style.

WINSFORD, THE VILLAGE 1930 83546

EXFORD, PARK STREET 1892 31196

CULBONE, THE SMALLEST PARISH CHURCH IN ENGLAND 1929 82194

CULBONE
The Smallest Parish Church in England 1929

Nearing the coast, in a steep wooded combe 400 feet above the sea, Culbone's church is well-known to walkers along the Somerset and North Devon Coast Path , but is inaccessible by public road. Partly Norman, it is reputedly the smallest regularly used church in England at 35 feet long. Its most unusual feature is the spire which rises straight from the nave roof, but its chief charm is its peaceful setting.

PORLOCK
The Foot of Porlock Hill 1923

Porlock Hill used to strike dread into the hearts of holiday-makers until relatively recently. Grinding up with slipping clutch and near-bursting radiators, it was, I recall, one of the trickiest parts of our summer holiday route in the 1950s to North Devon and Cornwall, with its hairpin bends and ascent of nearly 500 feet in a third of a mile.

PORLOCK, THE FOOT OF PORLOCK HILL 1923 75069

PORLOCK, GENERAL VIEW 1923 75034

This view, from Parson's Hill between the deep tree-filled Hawk Combe and the A39, looks across the small town below to Hurlstone Point. Between is the flat farmland running inland from Porlock Bay between the wooded northern edge of Exmoor's sandstone hills and the hills west of Minehead. Since 1923, Porlock has expanded to fill the fields between it and the line of prominent white houses.

PORLOCK, THE CHURCH 1907 58348

Porlock's church, dedicated to the 6th-century Welsh Celtic saint Dubricius, has a 13th-century tower with a later shingled spire which is curiously truncated. It is said locally that its top was cut off and removed in the 19th century to Culbone, where a short shingled spire rises from the nave roof (see picture 82194). Parsons Street, on the right, has some large Victorian houses looking over the churchyard.

PORLOCK, THE SHIP INN 1923 75036

The lanes and streets of Porlock wind delightfully between attractive whitewashed and thatched houses, including
The Ship Inn with its characteristic external chimney stack in the centre of the street front; the Lake poet William
Southey stayed here several times. These stacks are common in the West Country from medieval times to the 17th
century, and The Ship's has a good 16th-century round flue.

PORLOCK WEIR, THE FORESHORE 1929 82180

The sea has long retreated from Porlock village to the present seashore: it is now a mile and a half drive to its outlet to
the sea at Porlock Weir, a charming small harbour with three hotels as well as whitewashed cottages. In this view from
the harbour wall The Anchor Hotel is on the right, while the cottage on the left is today hidden by public lavatories.

BOSSINGTON, THE VILLAGE 1901 47385

Bossington, at the foot of Bossington Hill and on a loop road from the A39, merges with the hamlet of Lynch; it is a pretty village, with whitewashed sandstone rubble houses. Olands, the house on the left, has an external chimney-breast, thus making sure that neighbours knew the yeoman owner was wealthy enough to have a fireplace. The cottage on the right has one hidden by creeper.

WEST LUCCOMBE, THE VILLAGE 1901 47389

South of the A39, we climb from lush pastures towards Exmoor and the well-wooded Holnicote Estate and Dunkery Hill, much of which are owned by the National Trust. West Luccombe, a hamlet a good mile north-west of Luccombe itself, has some good cottages on the lane from Hawkcombe, with Inglenook on the left and the yellow ochre-washed Rose Tree Cottage on the right. Beyond is West Luccombe Farm.

LUCCOMBE, THE VILLAGE 1901 47394

Luccombe village itself is seen here against the backdrop of the wooded Horner Hill in a view taken from Knowle Top. Beyond the former school and schoolmaster's house is the church, dominated by its 15th-century tower which is over eighty feet high. The cottage to the right of the old school has a date plaque '1680'.

LUCCOMBE, THE VILLAGE 1901 47393

Down in this very picturesque village, the cottage beyond the lych gate has the village hall attached at the far end, all beneath a continuous thatched roof. To the left is Ketnor, Luccombe Post Office, a late 17th-century house with a good external stack. Ketnor is the name of former owners of the shop, and the name board survives today.

EXMOOR
Webber's Post 1923

From near Luccombe the road climbs through Horner Woods to Webber's Post on Luccombe Hill and onto the wildest parts of Exmoor. In 1923 the track weaving into the distance was unsurfaced, and the tourist felt he was indeed on the edge of a wilderness. Since then the trees have advanced somewhat into the foreground; the track to Watercombe is now tarmacked, as is the right-hand one, which descends into the East Water combe on its way to Exford.

BRATTON
The Village 1923

Once back to the A39, continue east, and about a mile west of Minehead, turn left to descend into Bratton, a tucked-away village with an excellent 15th-century manor house, Bratton Court, complete with a chapel and gatehouse. In this view we look past Step Cottage with its external stack (now no longer with a thatched roof) towards the ford in the valley bottom. Frith photographers obviously liked those cottages with chimney-breasts on the street front.

EXMOOR, WEBBER'S POST 1923   75004

BRATTON, THE VILLAGE 1923   75017

BICKNOLLER, THE VILLAGE 1940 89022

CROWCOMBE, THE CROSS AND THE CAREW ARMS 1929
82121

BICKNOLLER
The Village 1940
Beyond Williton, our route follows the western edge of the Quantock Hills back towards Taunton. Geologically this ridge is the same as Exmoor, but rises only to 1200 feet or so. Along its steeper western face are a number of hamlets, including Bicknoller, at whose village inn Coleridge often drank at the end of a walk over the hills from Nether Stowey. The house on the left in Church Lane has recently been rethatched.

CROWCOMBE
The Cross and the Carew Arms 1929
Further south, Crowcombe is the largest village on the western flanks of the Quantocks, and once was a small market town. In the park to its north is Crowcombe Court, a Georgian country house built in the 1720s and 1730s for Thomas Carew. It is in brick, rather than stone, but cannot easily be seen from the village. Near the entrance to the main drive is this fine medieval market cross; beyond is the 18th-century Carew Arms, now with its render removed.

TRISCOMBE
Will's Neck 1929

Past Crowcombe's fine parish church, turn left onto a narrow lane that winds to Triscombe. Here the lane descends to the hamlet past Triscombe Farm with its thatched barn. Beyond is Will's Neck, the highest point in The Quantocks at 1261 feet, its bare bracken-clad flanks now clad with trees advancing higher up from the valley.

TRISCOMBE
The Blue Ball Inn 1906

In this view the photographer looks north from the lane that skirts Will's Neck. On the left is Tally Ho Cottage, now somewhat altered, and to the right The Blue Ball Inn, which occupies both ranges of cottages. At the left is the thatched barn of Triscombe Farm, seen in photograph No 82112, and a track starting its climb to the path that runs along the spine of the Quantocks.

TRISCOMBE, WILL'S NECK 1929 82112

TRISCOMBE, THE BLUE BALL INN 1906 55778

DODINGTON, THE HALL 1929 82141

The route diverts briefly to the east side of the Quantocks to visit Dodington, a small and peaceful hamlet just north of the busy A39. Next to the small 15th-century parish church, out of view to the right, is Dodington Hall, a long Elizabethan manor house of 1581. Partly bare stone and partly whitewashed, and with numerous stone-mullioned windows, its cross passage is behind the two-storey porch. If the back and front doors are open, you can see right through the house to the back garden.

NETHER STOWEY, THE POST OFFICE AND THE CROSS 1935 86626

In Nether Stowey, you are in Samuel Taylor Coleridge country: he rented a cottage in Lime Street from 1796; whilst here, he wrote 'The Ancient Mariner' and 'Kubla Khan', the latter famously interrupted by the visitor from Porlock. Here, at the junction of St Mary Street and Castle Street on the right, which leads to the Norman castle ruins, is the Clock Tower of 1897 topped by its timber belfry and weathervane.

Seaside Somerset:
Old Ports and Seaside Resorts

MINEHEAD
The Beach 1906 57157
Once a port described by Daniel Defoe as 'fairer, and much deeper, than those at Watchet and Porlock', it turned into a major seaside bathing resort in the later 19th century. Today, of course, it has Butlins Holiday Camp to support its holiday trade. Beyond the bathing machines, the newer town is on the left, the white cottages of Quay Town are on the right, and the old town climbs the hill towards the medieval church with its tall 15th-century tower.

MINEHEAD, THE CHURCH AND STREET c1879 12428
Our brief tour of Minehead starts up in Higher Town, the old town. Here the narrow Church Steps wind from
Vicarage Road up steps to the church at the town's summit. On the left corner is John's Cottage, a late 16th-century
stone house with a surviving moulded timber mullioned window facing the photographer. The Bridgwater pantiles
have been replaced, and Old Lantern on the right has had its thatch replaced by slates.

MINEHEAD, THE OLD TOWN 1890 27504

Quay Town, along the old harbour quays, has been much changed since 1890. To make a promenade, all the cottages on the sea side of the lane have been demolished: a great loss of character. Of those on the left, only the cottages in the distance survive; the middle distance cottages were replaced by an Arts and Crafts style pub, The Red Lion, not long after this view was taken.

MINEHEAD, QUAY STREET 1903 49644

By 1903, the Red Lion, seen on the far left, has replaced a row of fishermen's cottages, but those beyond mostly survive, one being now The Old Harbour House Tea Rooms. Behind are spectacularly steep pine-clad hills. All the stone walls on the right went for the promenade extensions, but I suppose one should be grateful that Minehead's rebuilding mania did not sweep all of the town's seafaring past away.

MINEHEAD
The Parade 1892 31223
The new seaside resort was mostly laid out south of the old town on
flatter land between the Lower Town, largely destroyed by fire in
1791, and the sea. The branch railway from Taunton spurred the
resort's growth; the station is now the terminus of the West
Somerset Railway, closed in 1971 but reopened in 1976 as a
preserved line. This view of The Parade, the centre of the new
development, gives an idea of its austere late Victorian qualities,
now much brightened by garish modern shopfronts.

DUNSTER
From the Park 1903 50472
Dunster Castle, set in its beautiful parkland, emerges from its
tree-girt ridge as one of the most picturesque compositions in
Somerset. Now owned by the National Trust, it was the home of
the Luttrell family for six centuries. The Norman gatehouse
from the town survives, but most of what you see now is the
1860s remodelling of the parts left after Civil War damage of the
castle and its Elizabethan and Jacobean reconstruction. Anthony
Salvin thoroughly medievalised the buildings to their present
romantic appearance.

DUNSTER, THE NUNNERY 1903 50477

Dunster is one of the most picturesque of Somerset's small towns; its long Market Place rises from the Yarn Market, or market cross, an octagonal structure of 1589, to the castle gatehouse with the castle looming beyond. Here the road turns right into Church Street with The Nunnery, a fine 14th-century three-storey town house with slate-hung jettied upper storeys. Beyond is Dollons House, stucco-fronted, and behind it can be seen the church tower, built in 1443.

BLUE ANCHOR, THE BEACH 1935 87049

After the historic riches of Dunster we descend, physically as in other ways, to Blue Anchor Bay, a seaside resort with a long beach and little character. There are numerous caravan parks and few buildings of any quality, but towards the east the land climbs towards Cleeve Hill and things become a little more scenic. At the west end of Blue Anchor there is a station on the West Somerset Railway.

OLD CLEEVE, GENERAL VIEW 1930 83554

On our route towards Watchet we move inland to Old Cleeve, a village grouped round a triangle of narrow steep lanes and amazingly secluded. This view, from east of the church, looks towards Minehead; now the white pavilions of Minehead Butlins glow like intrusive whited sepulchres in the distance. A will of 1533 left money to build the church tower.

WATCHET, THE HARBOUR 1927 80596

Watchet was one of medieval Somerset's most important towns, and its harbour remained important into the 20th century, exporting iron ore from the Brendon Hills to the south. This view, from the east side of the harbour, looks across the Esplanade to the slipway at the junction of Market Street and Swain Street, the old core of the town. The hills behind have not been built over - most expansion has been to the left of the viewpoint.

WATCHET, THE OLD MARKET HOUSE 1929 82097

At the centre of the town is the old Market House with its shallow arched openings and weather-vaned bellcote. It appears to date from about 1840, and houses an interesting museum, focusing on the town's long maritime history. At the far end of the building is the Court Leet Lock-Up, and a notice reminds the visitor that Coleridge apparently used Watchet as the port where his Ancient Mariner 'stoppeth one of three'.

WATCHET
Swain Street 1906 56800

Swain Street runs south from the harbour; it is narrow and mixed
architecturally, as can be seen in this Edwardian view. The best
house is on the right, slightly set back from the road and with a
central niche containing an urn. Built about 1835, it became a
bank, hence its current name 'The Old Bank House'. Many of the
buildings here were rebuilt during the late Victorian phase of
Watchet's industrial prosperity, and are not as picturesque as are
some Somerset townscapes.

DONIFORD, GENERAL VIEW 1927 80607

This attractive view from just behind the hamlet of Doniford looks along the bay towards the low Lias cliffs that partly conceal Watchet. In the distance is the more massive sandstone bulk of Greenaleigh Point beyond Minehead. It is quite a panorama; on land to the left, the West Somerset railway curves away from the coast, crossed by the road to Watchet.

ST AUDRIES, THE SCHOOL 1903 50459

St Audries occupies a natural bowl looking out over the sea above the cliffs of St Audries Bay. The main A39 skirts its southern edge, and you can catch a glimpse of it from the drive. A Victorian Tudor-style 'baronial pile', it is now the Amithaba Buddhist Centre; for some years it was a school, as in this view.

ST AUDRIES, THE WATERFALL 1903 50464
East and to the left of this view, the St Audries Bay Holiday Club occupies the cliff tops at the end of a winding lane that descends from the main road. This waterfall terminates the course of a stream that crashes onto St Audries' beach from the cliffs: such picturesque natural phenomena were popular with Frith photographers.

BURNHAM-ON-SEA
THE BEACH 1913 65386
Moving further east along Somerset's coast and across the River Parrett, we reach Burnham on Sea, in effect on the east side of the river's estuary. Nowadays it has views north-west to Steep Holm island and depressing views west to the troubled Hinckley Point nuclear power station. This 1913 view, though, captures the more carefree and innocent holiday atmosphere before amusement arcades and the like arrived.

BURNHAM ON SEA, THE PROMENADE 1907 58691
At the north end of the promenade the domestic character survives better than in the next two photographs. Beverley Cottage of the 1850s has a battlemented parapet, and beyond are two crescents, each flanking the junction of the promenade with Sea View Road. They date from 1855, and represent an attempt to give the resort an architecturally-planned seafront layout.

BURNHAM ON SEA, THE BEACH 1913 65379
Looking southwards, the view is terminated by the elaborately Italianate Queens Hotel. From the plain late Georgian-character stuccoed terraces, the architecture gets more seaside Victorian, with a profusion of bay windows and the use of various building stones; the four gabled houses date from 1897. The sea wall, recently here completed in reinforced concrete, has since been robustly and massively replaced to repel rising sea levels.

BURNHAM ON SEA, THE PROMENADE 1918 68565

This view looks north from the corner of Pier Street past the Queens Hotel, now painted to protect the rapidly-eroding stone work, towards the short pier; its pavilion-roofed structure is now named The Pavilion and houses amusement arcades, cafes and the like. The stone balustrades and small front gardens have all gone, and there are modern projecting single-storey frontages beyond the Queens Hotel for Sun Spot Amusements.

BREAN, THE POST OFFICE STORES c1960 B832043

All the way north from Burnham to Brean Down, the six miles of road behind the sand dunes and beaches has a string of bungalows, chalets, shops, caravan parks, amusement parks and holiday camps, as well the odd older building, including Berrow's medieval church in the dunes. Brean's Post Office and Stores is still here, although it is now a Spar shop, and the 1920s Methodist Church beyond is still busy on a Sunday.

BREAN DOWN 1918 68587

EAST BRENT, THE CHURCH 1961 E61012

BREAN DOWN 1918

It is a relief to reach the archaeologically rich and beautiful headland of Brean Down, a carboniferous limestone outlier of the Mendips reaching 300 feet high, from whose bare grassy slopes are long views to Wales, Glastonbury and along the Somerset coast. Closer in, you can look down on Weston Bay and Weston-super-Mare to the north: it is probably better not to look too closely at the holiday sprawl along the road back to Burnham-on-Sea.

EAST BRENT
The Church 1961

Heading back towards Highbridge and the end of this seaside tour, we head for East Brent on the north-east side of Brent Knoll; this is an Upper Lias limestone outlier rising steeply from the flat lands surrounding it. East Brent's church has a tall, slender spire, but its most remarkable feature is the nave ceiling of 1637 which has a sinuous pattern of imitation vault ribs focusing on three pendant bosses done in a Gothic revival style.

BRENT KNOLL 1903 50176

The Knoll, rising 550 feet from the Somerset flatlands between the Rivers Axe and Brue, is topped by one of Somerset's finest Iron Age hill forts. The sides of the Knoll are fringed with medieval strip linchets, or terraces, formed for ploughing very steep slopes. Brent Knoll village straggles along the western side of the Knoll, with St Michael's Church, a dedication often associated with hill-tops and hills, to the centre and the Manor House of the 1860s to the right.

BRENT KNOLL, THE VILLAGE 1913 65392

This lane leads from the main through road to the church and Manor House. The house on the left has been demolished, and the lane now has modern houses on both sides. The church with its elegant 15th-century west tower is well worth visiting for its medieval woodwork, including the benches and roofs.

HIGHBRIDGE, CHURCH STREET 1903 50173

Chapter 2's tour finishes at Highbridge, not one of Somerset's most attractive towns. This view looks along Church Street from its junction with Market Street and Tylers Way; the latter is a modern road and where the boys stand is now a roundabout. The George Hotel on the right with the porch survives, but the branch railway line to Burnham-on-Sea, its level crossing gates shown closed, has long gone.

HIGHBRIDGE, THE RIVER BRUE 1903 50175

South of the town, beyond the stock market, the Bridgwater Road crosses the River Brue, here canalised. The Brue drains a major section of the Somerset Levels to Glastonbury and beyond; the Victorian sluices in the distance are a vital part of maintaining water levels and preventing flooding of the low-lying countryside. The cottages along the bank date from 1877 onwards, with two further pairs added in 1909 in the middle distance gap.

The Mendips to Frome

COMPTON BISHOP
The Village and Crooks Peak 1907 58713

This route heads for the beautiful Mendip Hills, the carboniferous limestone ridge
that separates the Avon valley and Bath and Bristol from the rest of Somerset.
Their character is very different from the Quantocks or Exmoor; here, sheep
scratch an existence from the poor limestone soils, and the fields are divided by
dry stone walls. The Mendips rise to over 1000 feet, very steeply on the west side.
Compton Bishop is at the western end on the slopes of a combe.

COMPTON BISHOP, CROOKS PEAK GUEST HOUSE c1960 C147014
To the west of Compton Bishop, the former Crooks Peak Guest House is now a private house, almost invisible behind high beech hedges. Built about 1910, the guest house served walkers and holiday makers, and its name refers to the 625 foot peak behind the house. The guest house also gave splendid views south across the levels towards Exmoor.

AXBRIDGE, THE SQUARE c1955 A254058
Behind this ancient market town, the Mendips rise steeply, while the long main street of Axbridge winds to and from the central market place. It retains its medieval plan and character remarkably with tall houses lining its narrow street, many of them timber-framed and jettied, including King John's Hunting Lodge on the left; it is a house of about 1500, now a museum, with its fine timber-framing exposed and owned by the National Trust. The Old Angel on the right is also 16th-century and jettied.

CHEDDAR, THE GORGE c1873 6984
Without doubt, Cheddar Gorge is the most spectacular natural phenomenon in South-west England. The gorge cuts its way out of the carboniferous limestone as if it was in the Peak District of Derbyshire; it is an underground cavern whose roof has collapsed, leaving soaring cliffs and crags of unsurpassed grandeur. Note the Frith photographer's dwarfed carriage waiting patiently far below.

CHEDDAR
THE VILLAGE c1873 6982

In 1873, this wonder of nature had a quarrymen's village at its entrance. The cottages on the left remain beyond the millpond; the row behind were built in 1667 and are now the Cheddar Toy and Model Museum. The house on the bend is now Derrick's Tea Rooms and Restaurant, but the cottages on the right went for road widening. Beyond now is an 1933 International Modern-style flat-roofed restaurant, besides other modern cafes and souvenir shops.

CHEDDAR, THE VILLAGE 1908 60145

CHEDDAR, THE VILLAGE 1908 60151

CHEDDAR
The Village 1908
Of the houses and cottages in this view, only the slate-roofed row with the chimney smoke survives. The lane leads to the White Hart, which does remain, but it is out of picture round the corner. The winding narrow lanes are still a problem in high summer, of course, but it seems that the village has needlessly lost a lot of its original houses and cottages.

***

CHEDDAR
The Village 1908
This view of quarrymen's cottages is an echo of a long-gone past for this area. It is now very much a tourist mecca. Scenes like these have been submerged by new building and the impedimenta of servicing tourism: cafes, souvenir shops, car parks, public conveniences and other facilities.

CHEDDAR
Glen Middle Mill 1908

If Sally Spencer, the lady looking at the photographer, came back today, she would see that almost all in this view (except the rear block of Pavey's Temperance Hotel) has been demolished since 1908, partly for road widening to cope with Cheddar's enormous volume of tourists. A remnant of the outbuilding on the left is incorporated in Fortes Ice Cream Parlour. Pavey's rear block is now Old Rowlands, selling pottery.

CHEDDAR
The Cliff Hotel 1908

The Cliff Hotel, recommended by the Cycle Touring Club in 1908 (their wheel symbol is mounted beside a first floor window), is now Cox's Mill Hotel; it has been extended over the off licence to the left and into the buildings to the right. The door hood has also been removed - presumably it was hit too often by motor coaches heading for the main caves and the Gorge. The buildings on the right have long gone.

CHEDDAR, GLEN MIDDLE MILL 1908   60144

CHEDDAR, THE CLIFF HOTEL 1908   60131

WEDMORE
Church Street c1955 W169001
We head away from Cheddar to Wedmore, a small town in the fork
of a valley on the north side of the ridge that stretches west from
Wells. It looks across the Levels to the Mendips. It is known to
history students as a royal residence and the setting for King
Alfred's meeting in 878 with Guthrum, the leader of the all-
conquering Danish armies. The resulting Treaty of Wedmore
divided England into two: the Danes were ceded all the territory
east of Watling Street, the 'Danelaw'.

WOOKEY HOLE, THE WITCH 1896 38939

The route then heads east back to the Mendips to visit another celebrated tourist attraction, Wookey Hole. Underground caverns hollowed out by streams are a feature of carboniferous limestone country, and Wookey Hole is one of the more spectacular examples. Here, the visitor sees a sequence of splendidly named caves, including the Witches Kitchen, the Great Hall and Cathedral Cavern. It is also the source of the River Axe, which powered the nearby Victorian paper mill, now also a museum, restaurant and shop.

WELLS, HIGH STREET C1955 W47051

Wells is, of course, famed for its superb cathedral and the Bishop's Palace. The town is also a very fine one, with much of its medieval plan intact. Indeed, many of the Georgian and 19th-century facades in the High Street, which winds uphill towards the market place, conceal medieval and later timber-framed buildings.

WELLS

MARKET PLACE 1890 23894
Little has changed here: the cannon
has gone, and the buildings between
the gatehouses now have dormers. The
1793 fountain remains, while the
Georgian bay windows to the range
beyond conceal Bishop Bekynton's mid
15th-century Nova Opera, a range of
houses over workshops and shops built
along the north side of the market
place. Their fine timber roofs remain,
and in this view you can see two of the
medieval stepped buttresses. Beyond
'Davy's' are the gables and oriels of the
15th-century Crown Hotel.

WELLS, THE CATHEDRAL, WEST FRONT 1923 73993

WELLS
The Cathedral, West Front 1923

The glory of the city is undoubtedly its cathedral. The diocese was founded here in 909 AD, and the present church replaced a Norman one consecrated in 1148. The building started in the 1180s and was finished by the late 1230s; the external climax is the west front screen, which has over 400 carved figures in its niches. Above are 14th-century west towers, and beyond the great central tower soars, which can be seen from many locations in the low-rise town and beyond.

SHEPTON MALLET
The Cross 1899

Five miles east of Wells in the eastern Mendips, Shepton Mallet was a prosperous wool manufacturing town, which declined when northern England's Industrial Revolution got under way. The fine market cross at the entrance to the Market Place has an elaborate medieval polygonal centre, with three storeys of arched niches; the crocketed pinnacle emerges from a plainer arched surrounding structure of about 1700 (all was rebuilt in 1841).

SHEPTON MALLET, THE CROSS 1899 44097

SHEPTON MALLET
Town Street 1899 44843

In the 19th century, various industries were established to replace the wool cloth ones; these included brewing, with the splendidly named Anglo-Bavarian Brewery being established near Commercial Road. From the north-west corner of Market Place, Town Street descends the hill past a drapers, a dairy utensil manufacturer and a shoe shop, all three displaying their wares.

SHEPTON MALLET, HIGH STREET 1899 44841

The High Street approaches the Market Place from the south, slightly downhill beyond the crossroads in the middle distance. The west side of the Market Place is in the distance. Most of the houses have Georgian and early 19th-century fronts of harmonious proportions and scale, although there is a grander later Victorian bank building at the crossroads.

NUNNEY, THE CASTLE c1965 N52015

Heading east away from the Mendips onto the rolling eastern Somerset countryside, we reach Nunney. At the north end of the village is a tall oblong keep set in a neat moat with massive towers at each angle, which was licensed in 1373 for John de la Mare, Sheriff of Somerset. Now roofless and floorless, it was bombarded in 1645 during a Civil War siege. Beyond, in its lee, is the good early 18th-century Manor Farm House.

MELLS, FROM THE RIVER 1907 58873

Circling Frome, we head north to the Mells Stream valley and Mells village, the home of the Horners, the nursery rhyme Little Jack Horner's family. John Horner, bailiff to the last Abbot of Glastonbury before the Dissolution of the Monasteries under Henry VIII, managed to acquire the Abbey's Mells estates. Here the photographer looks across the Mells Stream to the village and the church.

MELLS, THE VILLAGE 1907 58872

The photographer is looking north-west downhill across the Mells Stream bridge to the village, an attractive cluster of stone houses with many thatched roofs. St Andrew's Church has one of the finest west towers in Somerset; it is early 16th-century, and over one hundred feet high, with three belfry windows side by side on each face above three blank ringing-chamber windows.

NORTON ST PHILIP, THE GEORGE INN c1950 N218001
Built in the late 14th century for the Carthusian monks of Hinton Priory, the George Inn catered for the wool merchants who came to the town's two annual fairs: it performed a useful service and was a source of income. This famous and most attractive inn has a stone ground floor and two jettied timber-framed upper storeys and fire-proof stone side elevations; on each gable are rare original lantern-like stone chimneys.

RODE, THE VILLAGE c1960 R406012
Rode church is at the south-east end of the village, the bulk of which is to the north-west towards the River Frome. This view was taken from the south-west. The A361 Frome to Trowbridge road separates St Laurence's church, with its rugged and battlemented 15th-century west tower, from the rest of the village.

BECKINGTON, RAVENSCROFT SCHOOL c1955 B402004

A fine stone village a mile from Frome, Beckington has some superb stone houses and a church with an excellent Norman tower. The Castle, in 1955 the Ravenscroft School, a boys' prep school, is a late 16th-century house of three storeys with gabled attics and a three-storey porch and stair turret, both crowned with medieval-style battlements.

FROME, MARKET PLACE 1907 58843

The town, built in oolitic limestone, is a most attractive one: its streets curve up and down hill picturesquely. Like Shepton Mallet and other southern cloth towns, it prospered until the woollen industry moved to Lancashire and Yorkshire's new mills after 1800 - thus in effect preserving the town for us architecturally through economic decay. Here, the Georgian character of the more formal Market Place is clear, descending to the bridge over the Frome.

FROME

Cheap Street 1907 58850

Cheap Street, off Market Place and now pedestrianised, retains its medieval and Tudor character: it has a stream running down its centre in a channel. This view looks uphill towards the Market place. On the right is a late Tudor jettied timber-framed house, and opposite Vincent the Fishmonger's building survives as The Settle Bakehouse, Restaurant and Tea Rooms..

FROME

The Oldest House 1907 58851

At the south end of Cheap Street, seen on the right, were the premises of H R Hughes; the building has a narrow three-sided front and a stone-tiled roof, also with three planes. Grape Nuts, Bovril and Rowntrees Cocoa give a clue as to his produce, sold from what Frith called the oldest house in Frome. To the left, Eagle Lane climbs towards the west end of the Market Place.

FROME, BATH STREET 1907 58844
Much grander is Bath Street. Its name is appropriate, as its architecture is perhaps reminiscent of some of the later 18th-century parts of Bath itself. It curves uphill from the west end of Market Place south towards the parish church with Georgian facades stepping up the gradient, some on the right linked by ramped cornices.

FROME

Christ Church Street 1907 58847

From the evidence of these ornate High Victorian villas, with their William Butterfield-style Gothic architecture phasing into more Italianate styles in the distance, Frome's economy successfully diversified after the decline of its woollen cloth industry into other industries, such as printing. This view completes the tour of The Mendips and Frome area.

Central Somerset:
The Levels or Moors

BRIDGWATER
The Market and the Church 1890 27899
We now embark on a tour of the Moors or Levels, the vast flat
lands of central Somerset, where great drains and canalised rivers
keep the marshes at bay. We start at Bridgwater, a prosperous
industrial and commercial town with a fine historic core. Its
architectural focus is the domed Market Hall and St Mary's Church
with its tall spire emerging from a somewhat squat tower.

BRIDGWATER

HIGH STREET 1913 65364

To the left is the side elevation of the Market Hall, and to the right The Royal Clarence Hotel; this is of about 1835, with tall first-floor sash windows and a columned porch. It is now no longer an hotel, but shops with offices above. The cab rank and shelter have, of course, gone; further along to the right is now the grossly porticoed entrance to the Angel Place Shopping Centre.

BRIDGWATER, THE MARKET AND THE ROYAL CLARENCE HOTEL 1902 48709

By 1900, the citizens had erected a statue in front of the Market Hall of the great Admiral Blake, who was born in Bridgwater in 1598. This has now been moved to the High Street, so we have a clear view of the amateur architect John Bowen's rather good 1834 Market Hall: it has a columned semi-circular portico with above it a drum, dome and elegant lantern cupola.

BRIDGWATER, VIEW ACROSS THE BRIDGE 1890 27898

Fore Street heads east from the Market Place to cross the River Parrett on the iron bridge dated 1883; this replaced an early Coalbrookdale cast-iron bridge of 1795. Since 1890, there has been much change here; on the left hand side are nasty 1960s rebuilds, and several others have been rebuilt on the right. The curved-fronted Lloyds Wine and Spirit Vaults remain, now a building society, as does the gabled Starkey and Knight, now The Fountain pub.

BRIDGWATER, THE BRIDGE 1902 48712

Here the River Parrett heads towards the sea. Bridgwater was an important port, with railway docks and the terminus of the Taunton and Bridgwater Canal. Its well-known corrugated clay pantiles were widely used, shipped by barge and railway wagon. This view looks east into Eastover to the more industrial part of Bridgwater; unfortunately, J Sander's grandiose 1880s corner-turreted building has gone. Its replacement is truly dire, but York House on the left survives.

WEMBDON, THE CHURCH 1906 55790

The western suburbs of Bridgwater grew in the late 19th century to incorporate the village of Wembdon, whose church was at the far east end of the village. In 1906 it looks remarkably rural. Much of this feeling remains today: the churchyard wall with its railings and gates is unchanged, although the copper beech behind the left gate pier has grown very large.

OTHERY, MAIN ROAD c1955 O102009

From Bridgwater we head south-east into Sedgemoor to Othery, a village built on a low hill that rises 60 feet above the Moors. The main A361 Taunton road loops through the village, with the church in the back lane. This view looks south-west along the A361. The former Congregational Chapel, with a reused date plaque of 1836, was rebuilt about 1883 when the hall beyond was added

OTHERY, THE CHURCH c1955 O102007

The fine Perpendicular Gothic 15th-century crossing tower dominates the church. The photographer is facing the chancel. The unusual niche below the belfry openings for once retains its original statue. To the right the 19th-century Church Rooms, also in stone, survive, but all else in the view has gone; the thatched cottage has been replaced by bungalows!

BURROW BRIDGE, THE MUMP c1960 B839007
Two miles south-west of Othery, the Taunton Road skirts the Mump, a natural tor rising steeply from the surrounding Moors. Seen here from beyond the River Parrett, it once had a castle; now it is crowned by the altered medieval tower of St Michael's church, another example of this dedication on a hill site. Attached are the remains of a church started in 1724. The early 19th-century former rectory is on the left. The Mump is a remarkable landscape feature with echoes of Glastonbury Tor.

BURROW BRIDGE, KING ALFRED'S MONUMENT c1960 B839012
A mile south-west we come to Athelney, a name redolent of Anglo-Saxon history. The mound is crowned by a monument erected in 1801 to commemorate King Alfred's fortified base established here in 878 AD. From here he commenced the liberation of his Wessex kingdom from the Danish invading armies. At that time, of course, Athelney was an island in the marshes, and eminently defensible.

NORTH CURRY, THE SQUARE c1955 N219007
Continuing south-west, the route reaches North Curry, a village on the low ridge that separates West Sedge Moor from the Tone valley. Here in the centre of the village in the market place is a three-sided cross: three arches carry a spirelet, all in mellow golden limestone. Although it looks medieval, in fact it dates from 1897, and was erected to commemorate Queen Victoria's Diamond Jubilee.

NORTH CURRY, THE SMALLEST CINEMA IN ENGLAND c1965 N219014
Along Moor Lane is one of the types of view that appealed mightily to Frith's photographers. In this case it is the smallest cinema in England, formed by converting an outbuilding. In 1965 it was showing a John Wayne western. Now, however, it is a rendered annexe to Lantern Cottage beyond: it is a cinema no more.

LANGPORT, BOW STREET c1955 L365007

From North Curry, we skirt the south edge of West Sedge Moor to the town of Langport on the east bank of the River Parrett. Once a significant inland port, it has some fine houses and a Guildhall of 1733. Uphill, the town's east gate survives, with a chapel over it. This view looks out of the market place into Bow Street, which leads down to the river. Head's cycle shop on the right has now moved into the confectioners on the corner, and is an electrical shop.

HUISH EPISCOPI, ST MARY'S CHURCH c1955 H527051

Huish Episcopi stands at the confluence of the rivers Yeo and Parret. St Mary's Church has a fine example of a Somerset tower. The original tower was 13th-century, the body of the church is 16th- century

SOUTH PETHERTON, ST JAMES STREET C1960 S412007

Turning south, the tour reaches South Petherton, a small market town in the Lias limestone foothills. Its graceful parish church, dedicated to Saints Peter and Paul, is dominated, as is the town, by its octagonal crossing tower. Most houses are two-storey, and the archway on the left leads into St James Mews, a shopping centre. The cupola in the distance belongs to Blake Hall, part 18th-century but mostly of 1911.

MARTOCK, THE CROSS AND TOWN HALL 1900 45336

To the north-east is the charming market town of Martock with its triangular market place. The Market Cross, in fact a fluted Doric column surmounted by a sundial, was erected in 1741, not long after the Market Hall. Both are in golden Ham stone; the Market Hall has a Venetian first-floor window above the pedimented doorway. Manor Place, to the right, still has its magnolia tree, and the West Somerset Stores behind the Market Hall is now an estate agents.

MARTOCK, THE CHURCH 1900 45337

The main road turns past the imposing church, whose churchyard is entered by two 17th-century gateways. To the left are the arched and mullioned windows of the 1661 Almshouses; partly hidden is Ashlar House, which is mid 18th-century and set at the corner of Pound Lane, which leads to the moated Manor House. The medieval Treasurer's House, owned by the National Trust, is just out of view to the right, beside the creeper-clad house.

SOMERTON, THE MARKET CROSS 1904 52500

Heading back north, we cross the River Yeo and reach Somerton, another medieval market town, this time on a ridge in the Polden Hills and on the south bank of the River Cary, which weaves through the hills on its way to Sedgemoor. As befits its status, it has a Market Cross, rebuilt in 1673, incorporating most of the medieval masonry. In a parlous state in 1904, with drunken battlements, it has since been fully restored. The baker's delivery trap beyond stands outside Langler House.

SOMERTON, THE TOWN HALL AND THE CROSS 1906 55815

Alongside the Market Cross, and also in Blue Lias limestone with Ham stone dressings, is the Town Hall. It was built in the early 18th century, and is no longer a town hall - currently (May 2000) it is for sale. The parish church, St Michael's, with its fine octagonal tower, occupies the north side of the Market Place, which is effectively bisected by the through road to Frome.

SOMERTON, BROAD STREET 1904 52505

Broad Street is a later medieval planned extension of the market place, which is beyond the end houses. Oblong in shape, it is a fine wide street, its qualities emphasised by the lime trees along each side. Linden House, a later 19th-century insertion on the right with gabled upper windows, dwarfs the late 18th-century cottages to its right. On the left, the mullioned windows behind the dead tree belong to Craigmore House, built in about 1700.

SOMERTON, THE LONG SUTTON AND LANGPORT ROADS 1904 52504

West of the Market Square the road divides: the left hand road goes to Long Sutton, the right fork heads for Langport. J Manning's Posting Establishment, Cycle Depot and Fancy Stores, the centrepiece of this view, is now Tony's Fish and Chips, with a modern two-storey wing at the side. The thatched house in Langport Road was rebuilt in about 1910. Everything somehow looks less characterful, and more sanitised.

COMPTON DUNDON, THE WINDMILL HILL MONUMENT 1904 52522

En route to Street, divert to climb to Windmill Hill: here, a splendid monument commemorates the great British admiral, Sir Samuel Hood, who died in 1814. Atop the hill, it has a pedestal with inscription plaques on three sides and a relief of a naval battle on the fourth. The column has a drum top with a crest of alternating ship's sails and ship's sterns, a most unusual and striking composition.

STREET, THE CLOCK TOWER 1896 38388

Reaching Street, we are in 'company town', a town dominated by the shoe makers C and J Clark. It is therefore appropriate that we start at Clark's original factory, which fronts High Street. The first phase dates from 1829; it was greatly enlarged in 1857, and was rounded off with a splendid clock tower in 1897.

STREET, THE CRISPIN HALL 1896 38389

The Clarks were philanthropic Quakers, and William provided this splendid institute, The Crispin Hall, named after St Crispin, the patron saint of shoemakers, further south-west along the High Street. Built in craggy rubblestone in a Tudor-ish style, it was opened by John Bright, the great Quaker free-trader, fighter for universal suffrage and radical thinker, in October 1865. It is still Street's community centre, a cafe, and a craft shop.

STREET, HIGH STREET 1896 38386

This view looks south-west along the High Street. Beyond Crispin Hall, most of the houses and shops date from the Clark era, with the occasional much lower earlier cottages interspersed. The house on the left has been replaced by The Crispin Centre, a large shopping precinct. In part of the old factory there is now a shoe museum; it traces the history of shoes, as well as that of the Clarks factories.

GLASTONBURY, THE ABBEY FROM THE WEST 1927 80562

This chapter finishes with a flourish in Glastonbury, one of England's most historic smaller towns, a major centre of pilgrimage in the middle ages and still regarded by many as of mythic importance. The 'discovery' of King Arthur and Queen Guinevere's graves in the 12th century, and the legend of Joseph of Arimathea, Christ's uncle, founding the first Christian church in England were powerful draws, and the abbey was one of England's wealthiest. Here we look west from the Edgar Chapel to the crossing and nave beyond.

GLASTONBURY, THE ABBEY BARN 1896 38381
Beside the ruins of the great abbey church, various monastery buildings survive, including the famous 14th-century Abbot's Kitchen and the Abbey Barn. This splendid six-bay stone building has the symbols of the Four Evangelists in the gables and wagon porches. It was built for Abbot Bere around 1500, and is now a rural life museum.

GLASTONBURY, MARKET PLACE 1896 38371
The town was laid out north and west of the Abbey precincts, with the Market Place at the junction of High, Magdalen, Benedict and North Load Streets. Much of its life was tied to the pilgrim trade: the George and Pilgrim Hotel was built by the abbey in the 15th century to cater for pilgrims, a splendid survival. The market cross of 1846 echoes that of Shepton Mallet's medieval parts, and replaced one similar to that in Somerton. The Abbey gatehouse is out of view to the right.

GLASTONBURY
High Street 1909 61542

The High Street runs parallel to the north wall of the Abbey precinct and has a good range of Georgian and early 19th-century two- and three-storey houses. Since 1909, Brooks and Sons and the house to its left have been demolished, and the Arches Way road formed. To the right, the finial belongs to The Avalon Club of 1897. Behind the photographer to the left is another Perpendicular town house, The Tribunal, the Abbot's court house, with a front of about 1500.

GLASTONBURY, ST BENEDICT'S STREET 1909 61543

Benedict Street leads west to Glastonbury's other surviving medieval parish church. It was rebuilt in about 1520 by Abbot Bere. The Great India and China Tea Company, an 1880s building (on the left) is now, aptly, the Mocha Berry Cafe, while the haberdashers on the right is now The Grafton Cafe; both establishments reflect the role of the town in servicing, feeding and watering the huge numbers of tourists (and pilgrims) who visit the town.

GLASTONBURY, THE TOR 1896 38382A

East of the town and the Abbey, Glastonbury Tor rises abruptly to 525 feet above sea level from the 'island' above the Moors on which Glastonbury is built. A stiff climb, it is crowned by the 14th-century tower of St Michael's Church. The rest of the church has gone, but the views from the summit of the Tor are superb and long. The myths and legends associated with ancient Glastonbury reach their fitting climax here, far above the flat Somerset Levels spread out below.

South Somerset:
The Ham Stone Country

BRUTON
King Alfred's Tower c1955 B842013
The last tour heads west from the Wiltshire border to Devonshire; we are
never far from Dorset to the south. We start close to Stourhead, at King
Alfred's Tower. This has nothing to do with the Anglo-Saxon king, of course:
it was built by Henry Hoare of Stourhead in the 1760s as an eye-catcher, a
function its 150 feet serve well, as it can be seen from miles away.

BRUTON, PATWELL STREET c1955 B842011

Five miles west is Bruton, a town built mainly of Lias limestone, bisected by the River Brue. This was a notoriously dangerous river; many houses well uphill from it have flood markers, particularly from the 1917 flood. There is one on the Old Bull Inn in this view, at least 20 feet above normal river level. It is unusual that the shops along this winding road have been turned into houses, as has the Old Bull Inn.

CASTLE CARY, THE TOWN HALL c1960 C611061

West of Bruton, Castle Cary is set on the side of the oolite hills of southern Somerset, with Castle Cary Park on Lodge Hill rising steeply behind the church. The Market Hall in golden limestone is a curiosity architecturally; it dates from 1855 and replaces an earlier building of 1616, and is built in a not-quite-Gothic style. It now houses a museum of country and domestic life, the tourist information office and a dance studio. Beyond is the Roundhouse, or Lockup, built in 1779 for £23.

CASTLE CARY, FORE STREET c1955 C611006

There was a castle here, which was besieged by King Stephen in 1138, but its keep has long gone; only its outline is marked on the grass of its hill at the end of Bailey Street. In this view the photographer looks along Fore Street past The White Hart; on the opposite side of the road there is a raised pavement.

QUEEN CAMEL, CHURCH LANE c1955 Q18001

To the south-west, the tour reaches Queen Camel. Here the A359 Yeovil road goes through a series of right-angle bends through the village, south of the River Cam. Church Path leads east from the attractive main road through the village towards the tall west tower of St Barnabas' church. The oolitic limestone is everywhere here: walls, pavings and lane setts. The cottage on the left is, in fact, the south or rear elevation of the Mildmay Arms restaurant.

MILBORNE PORT, THE VILLAGE C1955 M180009

Milborne Port lies east of the Dorset town of Sherborne. It is noted for its parish church, which combines Anglo-Saxon detail and features with Norman work, a late 11th-century phase cumbersomely termed Saxo-Norman Overlap. It is a most interesting church; you will find it down a lane to the right off the busy London Road, the A30.

MILBORNE PORT, THE VILLAGE C1955 M180004

In this view we are looking north-west up London Road towards the Queens Head in the distance, beyond the junction with East Street. The pub has lost its Georgian door and pedimented hood for a more modern opening. The cottages on the right remain, but the right-hand one, Vine Cottage, has had its render removed and badly-proportioned stained-glass windows inserted.

MILBORNE PORT
Ven House c1955

Further downhill along London Road, Ven House is set back from the road beyond a forecourt. It is in English Baroque style: giant pilasters, cornice and attic are surmounted by a balustraded parapet. Started in 1698 and finished by 1730, it is built in brick with Ham stone dressings. Designed by Nathaniel Ireson, who also designed Crowcombe Court in The Quantocks for James Medlycott, it is a most elegant composition framed by the cedars.

MILBORNE PORT
The Village 1959

At the west end of the village, at the junction of Gainsborough Road with the A30, is this former school of the 1880s, built in rock-faced rubble stone and ashlar dressings. Now occupied by an engineering firm, it is an interesting composition with its 5-bay arcaded 'cloister', grand dormers and spired clock tower.

MILBORNE PORT, VEN HOUSE c1955 M180010

MILBORNE PORT, THE VILLAGE 1959 M180007

YEOVIL, MIDDLE STREET 1903 49166
Yeovil is by far the largest town in south Somerset. First chartered in 1209, its major industry was glove-making, using local sheepskin; Westland Aircraft is now the most important industry in this greatly-expanded town. The centre has suffered extensive redevelopment, nowhere more so than in this part of Middle Street; not a single building shown in the photograph survives, and the left side is now the shopping centre named Glovers Walk.

YEOVIL, MIDDLE STREET 1900 45309

Further uphill, more does survive - but not the Tudor jettied and timber-framed George Hotel, nor Frisbys. On the right Olivers, 'The Largest Retailer of Boots in the World', survives; it is still selling shoes as Timpsons. Beyond is now a 1960s Woolworths. Thus Middle Street has lost most of its historic character, and has utterly disappeared at its southern end.

YEOVIL, PRINCES STREET 1900 45310

Princes Street fares somewhat better, although the creeper-clad Georgian house beyond the shop on the right was rebuilt in 1950s Neo-Georgian. Whitby and Sons' shopfront has gone, as have most of the others in this view. Amid the stone and render, the pedimented corner building on the left is in brick, and was erected in 1885. At the junction with the High Street in the distance there is now a Millennium clock tower in Ham stone.

YEOVIL, THE PARK AND THE CHURCH 1900 45496

All the houses on the left went to make way for the inner ring road and its roundabout; the gable on the far right belongs to The Armoury pub, which does survive. The walls beyond went in 1924 for a building which is now a health and fitness club. The church tower in the distance is that of St John's parish church, a fine church of about 1400 with a 92 feet high tower.

BRYMPTON D'EVERCY, THE CHURCH AND THE HOUSE 1900 45329

Only about 2 miles from Yeovil's bustle, Brympton D'Evercy is in a completely tranquil setting approached along an avenue of plane trees. It is a stunning group: the medieval church, crowned by a most unusual lantern-like belfry; a 15th-century chantry or priest's house, now a museum; and the grand country house, all in golden Ham stone. The west front, seen here, is mainly Tudor, with mullioned and transomed windows and a battlemented stair turret and parlour bay at the left. It is all surpassingly beautiful.

MONTACUTE, MONTACUTE HOUSE 1900 45333

Heading north-west, the route reaches Montacute. A borough since around 1100, its name derives from St Michael's Hill to the west, in Latin 'mons acutus' or steep hill. It is a delightful Ham stone-built town, hardly larger now than a village. Montacute House lies to the north-east: it is a superb E-plan country house of the 1590s of three storeys. Its top-storey long gallery contains the Tudor collections of the National Portrait Gallery.

CREWKERNE, THE MARKET SQUARE c1955 C185031

Heading south-west towards Dorset we reach Crewkerne, another medieval market town that later specialised in sail-making for the Royal Navy until steam supplanted sail. It is a stone town, with one of the finest 15th-century churches in the county, largely built from the wool wealth of the town. This view in the Market Square gives a good idea of the town's high-quality Georgian and early 19th-century stone houses.

MISTERTON, THE POST OFFICE c1955 M360009

South-east of Crewkerne, past its factories and over the railway, is the village of Misterton, which lies along the A356 Dorchester road. R Sweet's shop is now painted white, and is the Misterton Post Office and Stores, while beyond is The Globe Inn. Helen Matthews, who wrote 'Coming Through the Rye', a Victorian novel not much read these days, was born in Misterton.

CHARD, HIGH STREET 1907 58761

Further west along the A30, Chard is a market town laid out in 1234 by Bishop Jocelyn of Wells. It grew into a prosperous wool town; in the 19th century cloth-making was replaced by lace-making and producing agricultural machinery. In this view, which looks east, the portico of the 1834 Town Hall dominates, with its two storeys of Tuscan columns, pediment and clock turret.

CHARD
OLD HOUSES, FORE STREET 1907
58766

Nearly opposite the Town Hall are two remarkable survivals from late Tudor times. These are two courtyard houses side by side; their fine porches lead into passages to small courtyards with halls across the rear - one is a first floor hall, once used as a court house. To the street, arched mullioned windows proliferate; shop fronts to the ground floor replace the Elizabethan merchants' workshop doors and windows.

CHARD, FORE STREET 1907 58762

At the bottom end of Fore Street, on the right, is another Elizabethan building: the old Grammar School of 1583, with its tall porch bay, now part of Chard School. The street curves uphill with a vigorously-flowing water channel alongside the road edge of each pavement. On the left, beyond the Methodist Church, is a house of 1900 with very early and rare concrete interlocking roof tiles set in a diagonal pattern.

BUCKLAND ST MARY, GENERAL VIEW c1960 B841007

As a break from a succession of market towns, the route heads north-west to Buckland St Mary, situated just north of the A303 and at the east end of the well-wooded Blackdown Hills. It is really a scattered hamlet with a church; its setting in the pastoral and wooded landscape of this area is most attractive.

BUCKLAND ST MARY
The Post Office c1960

Buckland St Mary Post Office is still a post office, but one wonders for how much longer. The only real change in this view is a bungalow built in the plot beside the car. Frith photographers certainly liked to take views of post offices, doubtless because the resulting postcards could be sold in them.

———

ILMINSTER
The Market Square 1907

The tour of southern Somerset concludes in Ilminster. The name means minster or church near the River Isle. The town, now more peaceful since the A303 bypass was completed, is mostly built in the warm golden Ham stone with Georgian and 19th-century frontages. Here we look down East Street towards the Market Hall; Silver Street is beyond, and the church tower can be glimpsed to the right.

BUCKLAND ST MARY, THE POST OFFICE c1960 B841001

ILMINSTER, THE MARKET SQUARE 1907 58745

ILMINSTER, THE MARKET PLACE c1955 17015

As we look back up East Street, the focus of the view is the Market Hall. Built in Ham stone (of course), it has a hipped slate roof carried on three shallow arches each side with Tuscan columns attached. It was built in 1813, but may be a replica of an earlier building; or it may incorporate earlier, probably 17th-century, material.

ILMINSTER, THE GRAMMAR SCHOOL 1907 58749

Positioned in the playing field of the school in Wharf Lane, our photographer looks towards the school buildings erected in 1878 in approved Gothic style. Modern buildings for the school, Greenfylde School, now occupy the playing field. Beyond is the late 15th-century church of St Mary; its superb west tower owes its scale and magnificence to the town's medieval wool prosperity, and is something of a copy of Wells Cathedral's sublime crossing tower.

Index

Frith Book Co Titles

www.francisfrith.co.uk

The Frith Book Company publishes over 100 new titles each year. A selection of those currently available is listed below. For latest catalogue please contact Frith Book Co.
Town Books 96 pages, approximately 100 photos. **County and Themed Books** 128 pages, approximately 150 photos (unless specified). All titles hardback with laminated case and jacket, except those indicated pb (paperback)

Amersham, Chesham & Rickmansworth (pb)	1-85937-340-2	£9.99	Devon (pb)	1-85937-297-x	£9.99
Andover (pb)	1-85937-292-9	£9.99	Devon Churches (pb)	1-85937-250-3	£9.99
Aylesbury (pb)	1-85937-227-9	£9.99	Dorchester (pb)	1-85937-307-0	£9.99
Barnstaple (pb)	1-85937-300-3	£9.99	Dorset (pb)	1-85937-269-4	£9.99
Basildon Living Memories (pb)	1-85937-515-4	£9.99	Dorset Coast (pb)	1-85937-299-6	£9.99
Bath (pb)	1-85937-419-0	£9.99	Dorset Living Memories (pb)	1-85937-584-7	£9.99
Bedford (pb)	1-85937-205-8	£9.99	Down the Severn (pb)	1-85937-560-x	£9.99
Bedfordshire Living Memories	1-85937-513-8	£14.99	Down The Thames (pb)	1-85937-278-3	£9.99
Belfast (pb)	1-85937-303-8	£9.99	Down the Trent	1-85937-311-9	£14.99
Berkshire (pb)	1-85937-191-4	£9.99	East Anglia (pb)	1-85937-265-1	£9.99
Berkshire Churches	1-85937-170-1	£17.99	East Grinstead (pb)	1-85937-138-8	£9.99
Berkshire Living Memories	1-85937-332-1	£14.99	East London	1-85937-080-2	£14.99
Black Country	1-85937-497-2	£12.99	East Sussex (pb)	1-85937-606-1	£9.99
Blackpool (pb)	1-85937-393-3	£9.99	Eastbourne (pb)	1-85937-399-2	£9.99
Bognor Regis (pb)	1-85937-431-x	£9.99	Edinburgh (pb)	1-85937-193-0	£8.99
Bournemouth (pb)	1-85937-545-6	£9.99	England In The 1880s	1-85937-331-3	£17.99
Bradford (pb)	1-85937-204-x	£9.99	Essex - Second Selection	1-85937-456-5	£14.99
Bridgend (pb)	1-85937-386-0	£7.99	Essex (pb)	1-85937-270-8	£9.99
Bridgwater (pb)	1-85937-305-4	£9.99	Essex Coast	1-85937-342-9	£14.99
Bridport (pb)	1-85937-327-5	£9.99	Essex Living Memories	1-85937-490-5	£14.99
Brighton (pb)	1-85937-192-2	£8.99	Exeter	1-85937-539-1	£9.99
Bristol (pb)	1-85937-264-3	£9.99	Exmoor (pb)	1-85937-608-8	£9.99
British Life A Century Ago (pb)	1-85937-213-9	£9.99	Falmouth (pb)	1-85937-594-4	£9.99
Buckinghamshire (pb)	1-85937-200-7	£9.99	Folkestone (pb)	1-85937-124-8	£9.99
Camberley (pb)	1-85937-222-8	£9.99	Frome (pb)	1-85937-317-8	£9.99
Cambridge (pb)	1-85937-422-0	£9.99	Glamorgan	1-85937-488-3	£14.99
Cambridgeshire (pb)	1-85937-420-4	£9.99	Glasgow (pb)	1-85937-190-6	£9.99
Cambridgeshire Villages	1-85937-523-5	£14.99	Glastonbury (pb)	1-85937-338-0	£7.99
Canals And Waterways (pb)	1-85937-291-0	£9.99	Gloucester (pb)	1-85937-232-5	£9.99
Canterbury Cathedral (pb)	1-85937-179-5	£9.99	Gloucestershire (pb)	1-85937-561-8	£9.99
Cardiff (pb)	1-85937-093-4	£9.99	Great Yarmouth (pb)	1-85937-426-3	£9.99
Carmarthenshire (pb)	1-85937-604-5	£9.99	Greater Manchester (pb)	1-85937-266-x	£9.99
Chelmsford (pb)	1-85937-310-0	£9.99	Guildford (pb)	1-85937-410-7	£9.99
Cheltenham (pb)	1-85937-095-0	£9.99	Hampshire (pb)	1-85937-279-1	£9.99
Cheshire (pb)	1-85937-271-6	£9.99	Harrogate (pb)	1-85937-423-9	£9.99
Chester (pb)	1-85937-382 8	£9.99	Hastings and Bexhill (pb)	1-85937-131-0	£9.99
Chesterfield (pb)	1-85937-378-x	£9.99	Heart of Lancashire (pb)	1-85937-197-3	£9.99
Chichester (pb)	1-85937-228-7	£9.99	Helston (pb)	1-85937-214-7	£9.99
Churches of East Cornwall (pb)	1-85937-249-x	£9.99	Hereford (pb)	1-85937-175-2	£9.99
Churches of Hampshire (pb)	1-85937-207-4	£9.99	Herefordshire (pb)	1-85937-567-7	£9.99
Cinque Ports & Two Ancient Towns	1-85937-492-1	£14.99	Herefordshire Living Memories	1-85937-514-6	£14.99
Colchester (pb)	1-85937-188-4	£8.99	Hertfordshire (pb)	1-85937-247-3	£9.99
Cornwall (pb)	1-85937-229-5	£9.99	Horsham (pb)	1-85937-432-8	£9.99
Cornwall Living Memories	1-85937-248-1	£14.99	Humberside (pb)	1-85937-605-3	£9.99
Cotswolds (pb)	1-85937-230-9	£9.99	Hythe, Romney Marsh, Ashford (pb)	1-85937-256-2	£9.99
Cotswolds Living Memories	1-85937-255-4	£14.99	Ipswich (pb)	1-85937-424-7	£9.99
County Durham (pb)	1-85937-398-4	£9.99	Isle of Man (pb)	1-85937-268-6	£9.99
Croydon Living Memories (pb)	1-85937-162-0	£9.99	Isle of Wight (pb)	1-85937-429-8	£9.99
Cumbria (pb)	1-85937-621-5	£9.99	Isle of Wight Living Memories	1-85937-304-6	£14.99
Derby (pb)	1-85937-367-4	£9.99	Kent (pb)	1-85937-189-2	£9.99
Derbyshire (pb)	1-85937-196-5	£9.99	Kent Living Memories(pb)	1-85937-401-8	£9.99
Derbyshire Living Memories	1-85937-330-5	£14.99	Kings Lynn (pb)	1-85937-334-8	£9.99

Available from your local bookshop or from the publisher

Frith Book Co Titles (continued)

Title	ISBN	Price	Title	ISBN	Price
Lake District (pb)	1-85937-275-9	£9.99	Sherborne (pb)	1-85937-301-1	£9.99
Lancashire Living Memories	1-85937-335-6	£14.99	Shrewsbury (pb)	1-85937-325-9	£9.99
Lancaster, Morecambe, Heysham (pb)	1-85937-233-3	£9.99	Shropshire (pb)	1-85937-326-7	£9.99
Leeds (pb)	1-85937-202-3	£9.99	Shropshire Living Memories	1-85937-643-6	£14.99
Leicester (pb)	1-85937-381-x	£9.99	Somerset	1-85937-153-1	£14.99
Leicestershire & Rutland Living Memories	1-85937-500-6	£12.99	South Devon Coast	1-85937-107-8	£14.99
Leicestershire (pb)	1-85937-185-x	£9.99	South Devon Living Memories (pb)	1-85937-609-6	£9.99
Lighthouses	1-85937-257-0	£9.99	South East London (pb)	1-85937-263-5	£9.99
Lincoln (pb)	1-85937-380-1	£9.99	South Somerset	1-85937-318-6	£14.99
Lincolnshire (pb)	1-85937-433-6	£9.99	South Wales	1-85937-519-7	£14.99
Liverpool and Merseyside (pb)	1-85937-234-1	£9.99	Southampton (pb)	1-85937-427-1	£9.99
London (pb)	1-85937-183-3	£9.99	Southend (pb)	1-85937-313-5	£9.99
London Living Memories	1-85937-454-9	£14.99	Southport (pb)	1-85937-425-5	£9.99
Ludlow (pb)	1-85937-176-0	£9.99	St Albans (pb)	1-85937-341-0	£9.99
Luton (pb)	1-85937-235-x	£9.99	St Ives (pb)	1-85937-415-8	£9.99
Maidenhead (pb)	1-85937-339-9	£9.99	Stafford Living Memories (pb)	1-85937-503-0	£9.99
Maidstone (pb)	1-85937-391-7	£9.99	Staffordshire (pb)	1-85937-308-9	£9.99
Manchester (pb)	1-85937-198-1	£9.99	Stourbridge (pb)	1-85937-530-8	£9.99
Marlborough (pb)	1-85937-336-4	£9.99	Stratford upon Avon (pb)	1-85937-388-7	£9.99
Middlesex	1-85937-158-2	£14.99	Suffolk (pb)	1-85937-221-x	£9.99
Monmouthshire	1-85937-532-4	£14.99	Suffolk Coast (pb)	1-85937-610-x	£9.99
New Forest (pb)	1-85937-390-9	£9.99	Surrey (pb)	1-85937-240-6	£9.99
Newark (pb)	1-85937-366-6	£9.99	Surrey Living Memories	1-85937-328-3	£14.99
Newport, Wales (pb)	1-85937-258-9	£9.99	Sussex (pb)	1-85937-184-1	£9.99
Newquay (pb)	1-85937-421-2	£9.99	Sutton (pb)	1-85937-337-2	£9.99
Norfolk (pb)	1-85937-195-7	£9.99	Swansea (pb)	1-85937-167-1	£9.99
Norfolk Broads	1-85937-486-7	£14.99	Taunton (pb)	1-85937-314-3	£9.99
Norfolk Living Memories (pb)	1-85937-402-6	£9.99	Tees Valley & Cleveland (pb)	1-85937-623-1	£9.99
North Buckinghamshire	1-85937-626-6	£14.99	Teignmouth (pb)	1-85937-370-4	£7.99
North Devon Living Memories	1-85937-261-9	£14.99	Thanet (pb)	1-85937-116-7	£9.99
North Hertfordshire	1-85937-547-2	£14.99	Tiverton (pb)	1-85937-178-7	£9.99
North London (pb)	1-85937-403-4	£9.99	Torbay (pb)	1-85937-597-9	£9.99
North Somerset	1-85937-302-x	£14.99	Truro (pb)	1-85937-598-7	£9.99
North Wales (pb)	1-85937-298-8	£9.99	Victorian & Edwardian Dorset	1-85937-254-6	£14.99
North Yorkshire (pb)	1-85937-236-8	£9.99	Victorian & Edwardian Kent (pb)	1-85937-624-X	£9.99
Northamptonshire Living Memories	1-85937-529-4	£14.99	Victorian & Edwardian Maritime Album (pb)	1-85937-622-3	£9.99
Northamptonshire	1-85937-150-7	£14.99	Victorian and Edwardian Sussex (pb)	1-85937-625-8	£9.99
Northumberland Tyne & Wear (pb)	1-85937-281-3	£9.99	Villages of Devon (pb)	1-85937-293-7	£9.99
Northumberland	1-85937-522-7	£14.99	Villages of Kent (pb)	1-85937-294-5	£9.99
Norwich (pb)	1-85937-194-9	£8.99	Villages of Sussex (pb)	1-85937-295-3	£9.99
Nottingham (pb)	1-85937-324-0	£9.99	Warrington (pb)	1-85937-507-3	£9.99
Nottinghamshire (pb)	1-85937-187-6	£9.99	Warwick (pb)	1-85937-518-9	£9.99
Oxford (pb)	1-85937-411-5	£9.99	Warwickshire (pb)	1-85937-203-1	£9.99
Oxfordshire (pb)	1-85937-430-1	£9.99	Welsh Castles (pb)	1-85937-322-4	£9.99
Oxfordshire Living Memories	1-85937-525-1	£14.99	West Midlands (pb)	1-85937-289-9	£9.99
Paignton (pb)	1-85937-374-7	£7.99	West Sussex (pb)	1-85937-607-x	£9.99
Peak District (pb)	1-85937-280-5	£9.99	West Yorkshire (pb)	1-85937-201-5	£9.99
Pembrokeshire	1-85937-262-7	£14.99	Weston Super Mare (pb)	1-85937-306-2	£9.99
Penzance (pb)	1-85937-595-2	£9.99	Weymouth (pb)	1-85937-209-0	£9.99
Peterborough (pb)	1-85937-219-8	£9.99	Wiltshire (pb)	1-85937-277-5	£9.99
Picturesque Harbours	1-85937-208-2	£14.99	Wiltshire Churches (pb)	1-85937-171-x	£9.99
Piers	1-85937-237-6	£17.99	Wiltshire Living Memories (pb)	1-85937-396-8	£9.99
Plymouth (pb)	1-85937-389-5	£9.99	Winchester (pb)	1-85937-428-x	£9.99
Poole & Sandbanks (pb)	1-85937-251-1	£9.99	Windsor (pb)	1-85937-333-x	£9.99
Preston (pb)	1-85937-212-0	£9.99	Wokingham & Bracknell (pb)	1-85937-329-1	£9.99
Reading (pb)	1-85937-238-4	£9.99	Woodbridge (pb)	1-85937-498-0	£9.99
Redhill to Reigate (pb)	1-85937-596-0	£9.99	Worcester (pb)	1-85937-165-5	£9.99
Ringwood (pb)	1-85937-384-4	£7.99	Worcestershire Living Memories	1-85937-489-1	£14.99
Romford (pb)	1-85937-319-4	£9.99	Worcestershire	1-85937-152-3	£14.99
Royal Tunbridge Wells (pb)	1-85937-504-9	£9.99	York (pb)	1-85937-199-x	£9.99
Salisbury (pb)	1-85937-239-2	£9.99	Yorkshire (pb)	1-85937-186-8	£9.99
Scarborough (pb)	1-85937-379-8	£9.99	Yorkshire Coastal Memories	1-85937-506-5	£14.99
Sevenoaks and Tonbridge (pb)	1-85937-392-5	£9.99	Yorkshire Dales	1-85937-502-2	£14.99
Sheffield & South Yorks (pb)	1-85937-267-8	£9.99	Yorkshire Living Memories (pb)	1-85937-397-6	£9.99

See Frith books on the internet at www.francisfrith.co.uk

FRITH PRODUCTS & SERVICES

Francis Frith would doubtless be pleased to know that the pioneering publishing venture he started in 1860 still continues today. A hundred and forty years later, The Francis Frith Collection continues in the same innovative tradition and is now one of the foremost publishers of vintage photographs in the world. Some of the current activities include:

Interior Decoration

Today Frith's photographs can be seen framed and as giant wall murals in thousands of pubs, restaurants, hotels, banks, retail stores and other public buildings throughout the country. In every case they enhance the unique local atmosphere of the places they depict and provide reminders of gentler days in an increasingly busy and frenetic world.

Product Promotions

Frith products are used by many major companies to promote the sales of their own products or to reinforce their own history and heritage. Frith promotions have been used by Hovis bread, Courage beers, Scots Porage Oats, Colman's mustard, Cadbury's foods, Mellow Birds coffee, Dunhill pipe tobacco, Guinness, and Bulmer's Cider.

Genealogy and Family History

As the interest in family history and roots grows world-wide, more and more people are turning to Frith's photographs of Great Britain for images of the towns, villages and streets where their ancestors lived; and, of course, photographs of the churches and chapels where their ancestors were christened, married and buried are an essential part of every genealogy tree and family album.

Frith Products

All Frith photographs are available Framed or just as Mounted Prints and Posters (size 23 x 16 inches). These may be ordered from the address below. From time to time other products - Address Books, Calendars, Table Mats, etc - are available.

The Internet

Already twenty thousand Frith photographs can be viewed and purchased on the internet. By the end of the year 2000 some 60,000 Frith photographs will be available on the internet. The number of sites is constantly expanding, each focussing on different products and services from the Collection.
The main Frith sites are listed below.
www.francisfrith.co.uk
www.frithbook.co.uk

See the complete list of Frith Books at:

www.frithbook.co.uk

This web site is regularly updated with the latest list of publications from the Frith Book Company. If you wish to buy books relating to another part of the country that your local bookshop does not stock, you may purchase on-line.

For further information, trade, or author enquiries please contact us at the address below:
The Francis Frith Collection, Frith's Barn, Teffont, Salisbury, Wiltshire, England SP3 5QP.
Tel: +44 (0)1722 716 376 Fax: +44 (0)1722 716 881 Email: uksales@francisfrith.com

See Frith books on the internet www.frithbook.co.uk

FREE PRINT OF YOUR CHOICE

Mounted Print
Overall size 14 x 11 inches (355 x 280mm)

Choose any Frith photograph in this book.
Simply complete the Voucher opposite and
return it with your remittance for £2.25 (to cover
postage and handling) and we will print the
photograph of your choice in SEPIA (size 11 x 8
inches) and supply it in a cream mount with a
burgundy rule line (overall size 14 x 11 inches).
**Please note: photographs with a reference
number starting with a "Z" are not Frith
photographs and cannot be supplied under
this offer.**
Offer valid for delivery to UK addresses only.

PLUS: **Order additional Mounted Prints
at HALF PRICE - £7.49 each** (normally £14.99)
If you would like to order more Frith prints from
this book, possibly as gifts for friends and family,
you can buy them at half price (with no
additional postage and handling costs).

PLUS: **Have your Mounted Prints framed**
For an extra £14.95 per print you can have your
mounted print(s) framed in an elegant polished
wood and gilt moulding, overall size 16 x
13 inches (no additional postage and handling
required).

IMPORTANT!

**These special prices are only available if you use
this form to order . You must use the ORIGINAL
VOUCHER on this page (no copies permitted). We
can only despatch to one address. This offer
cannot be combined with any other offer.**

Send completed Voucher form to:
**The Francis Frith Collection, Frith's Barn,
Teffont, Salisbury, Wiltshire SP3 5QP**

CHOOSE A PHOTOGRAPH FROM THIS BOOK

Voucher for **FREE** *and Reduced Price Frith Prints*

*Please do not photocopy this voucher. Only the original is valid,
so please fill it in, cut it out and return it to us with your order.*

Picture ref no	Page no	Qty	Mounted @ £7.49	Framed + £14.95	Total Cost
		1	Free of charge*	£	£
			£7.49	£	£
			£7.49	£	£
			£7.49	£	£
			£7.49	£	£
			£7.49	£	£
Please allow 28 days for delivery			* Post & handling (UK)		£2.25
			Total Order Cost		£

Title of this book . . . .

I enclose a cheque/postal order for £ . . . .
made payable to 'The Francis Frith Collection'

OR please debit my Mastercard / Visa / Switch (Maestro)
/Amex card
(credit cards please on all overseas orders), details below

Card Number

Issue No (Switch only)   Valid from (Amex/Switch)

Expires   Signature

Name Mr/Mrs/Ms . . . .
Address . . . .
. . . .
. . . .
. . . . Postcode . . . .
Daytime Tel No . . . .
Email . . . .

Valid to 31/12/07

Free Print – see overleaf

Would you like to find out more about Francis Frith?

We have recently recruited some entertaining speakers who are happy to visit local groups, clubs and societies to give an illustrated talk documenting Frith's travels and photographs. If you are a member of such a group and are interested in hosting a presentation, we would love to hear from you.

Our speakers bring with them a small selection of our local town and county books, together with sample prints. They are happy to take orders. A small proportion of the order value is donated to the group who have hosted the presentation. The talks are therefore an excellent way of fundraising for small groups and societies.

Can you help us with information about any of the Frith photographs in this book?

We are gradually compiling an historical record for each of the photographs in the Frith archive. It is always fascinating to find out the names of the people shown in the pictures, as well as insights into the shops, buildings and other features depicted.

If you recognize anyone in the photographs in this book, or if you have information not already included in the author's caption, do let us know. We would love to hear from you, and will try to publish it in future books or articles.

Our production team

Frith books are produced by a small dedicated team at offices in the converted Grade II listed 18th-century barn at Teffont near Salisbury, illustrated above. Most have worked with the Frith Collection for many years. All have in common one quality: they have a passion for the Frith Collection. The team is constantly expanding, but currently includes:

Paul Baron, Phillip Brennan, Jason Buck, John Buck, Ruth Butler, Heather Crisp, David Davies, Louis du Mont, Isobel Hall, Gareth Harris, Lucy Hart, Julian Hight, Peter Horne, James Kinnear, Karen Kinnear, Tina Leary, Stuart Login, David Marsh, Lesley-Ann Millard, Sue Molloy, Glenda Morgan, Wayne Morgan, Sarah Roberts, Kate Rotondetto, Dean Scource, Eliza Sackett, Terence Sackett, Sandra Sampson, Adrian Sanders, Sandra Sanger, Jan Scrivens, Julia Skinner, David Smith, Miles Smith, Lewis Taylor, Shelley Tolcher, Lorraine Tuck, Amanita Wainwright and Ricky Williams.